Loaded Cheesy Nachos Recipes

Pretty Perfect Nacho Dishes into Your Lap

By: Tyler Sweet

© 2021 Tyler Sweet, All Rights Reserved.

License Page

This book or any of its content may not be replicated by any means. Copying, publishing, distributing the contents of this publication without the explicit permission of the author is an infringement of the country's copyright law and will leave you liable to litigation. The contents of this book are well researched and fact-checked before printing to ensure that the readers get the best value. The author is not liable or responsible for the wrongful use of the information provided in the contents of this book.

Table of Contents

Introduction 6

    Carnitas Nachos 8

    Mac Nachos 11

    Grilled Nachos 14

    Apple Nachos 16

    Chipotle Nachos 18

    Keto Nachos 20

    Steak Nachos 23

    Veggie Nachos 26

    Greek Chicken Nachos 28

    Chicken Bell Pepper Nachos 30

    Irish Nachos 33

    Beef Nachos 36

    Chile Chicken Nachos 39

    BBQ Chicken Nachos 42

Mexican Nachos 44

Tuna Nachos 47

Fruit Nachos 49

Bean Nachos 52

Shrimp & Crabmeat Nachos 54

Chicken Enchilada Nachos 56

Cowboy Nachos 59

Chorizo Nachos 61

Traditional Nachos 64

Ravioli Nachos 66

Jackfruit Nachos 69

Pie Crust Nachos 72

Cajun Nachos 74

Fajita Nachos 77

Zucchini Nachos 79

Pumpkin Nachos 82

Conclusion 84

Biography 85

Author's Note 86

Introduction

Looking for cheesy nachos recipes with exciting loaded ingredients?

Here are 30 loaded cheesy nachos recipes to set you up with enchanting nachos recipes.

Who doesn't like nachos? From kids to the elderly, I think we all love these super versatile chips. These are crispy chips that treat best to your taste buds anywhere and everywhere.

There are so many ways you can enjoy nachos recipes like enjoy shrimp on the chips, or pumpkin on the chips. Best of all, based on ingredients, you can build your nachos recipes with lovely flavors and tastes.

Do you like spicy nachos? Then go for BBQ chicken nachos or Cajun nachos. If you want creamy and cheesy nachos, then go for chipotle nachos or mac nachos. The choices are endless and so is the fun.

Nachos have been the favorite of so many. But are you tired of making authentic recipes and want to make something fun and exciting? Then try these grilled nachos, chile chicken nachos, bean nachos, and chorizo for something unique and new to your taste buds.

These recipes have protein, veggies, cream, cheese, salsa, and a lot more to boost your mood on another level. There are several ways to make tortilla chips with seasoned meat, fruits, and rich cream poured on. It's one of the most ultimate foods that you can enjoy at home.

Remember, you don't need to be an expert to make Mexican delicacy at home. I have got you easy-to-follow recipes that guarantee the best taste, for your next party at home.

Enjoy these crunchy nachos recipes with your favorite dip to make a one-dish meal.

Carnitas Nachos

Carnitas nachos is a delicious recipe loaded with tasty ingredients like nachos chips, cheese, radishes, jalapeno peppers, seasoned pork, and hint of lemon. This dish looks extensive and is a tender snack to enjoy at home.

Serving Size: 4

Cooking Time: 4 hours

Ingredients:

- 2 lb. pork butt part, cut into pieces
- 4 tbsp butter, divided
- Salt, to taste
- 2 tsp chili powder
- 1 tsp cumin powder
- Black pepper, to taste
- 2 tbsp lime juice

For nachos

- 1 bag nachos chips
- 1 cup cheese
- 5 radishes, sliced
- 1 jalapeno pepper, sliced
- 1/2 cup sour cream
- 1 avocado, slices
- 1/4 cup cilantro, chopped

Instructions:

Cook pork pieces with butter in the frying pan.

Sprinkle chili powder, cumin powder, salt & pepper, and lime juice over the pork. Mix well.

Cook for 5 minutes. Then transfer the pork mixture in the slow cooker and cook for 4 hours.

Carnitas is done. Shred the pork.

Melt butter in the pan. Add shreeded pork and cook until crisp. Season with lime juice if needed.

Spread nachos chips on the serving plate. Top with carnitas, nacho cheese, radishes, avocado, cilantro, and jalapeño pepper.

Carnitas nachos is ready.

Mac Nachos

Mac nachos is cheesy indulgent with great sauce and baked. It gets ready in just 30 minutes with nachos, melted cheese, and tangy spicy sauce. A great snack idea for the evening!

Serving Size: 6

Cooking Time:35Minutes

Ingredients:

- 1 lb. ground beef
- 1 tsp garlic powder
- Salt and pepper, to taste
- 14 oz nachos chips
- 1 onion, chopped
- 1 cup lettuce, shredded
- 10 cheese slices
- Sesame seeds, for garnishing

For sauce

- 3/4 cup mayonnaise
- 3 tbsp yellow mustard sauce
- 1 tbsp tomato ketchup
- 2 tsp apple cider vinegar
- 1 tbsp pickle relish
- 1/2 tsp garlic powder
- 1/2 tsp onion powder
- 1/4 tsp paprika
- Salt, to taste

Instructions:

Preheat oven to 425°F.

Lines foil paper on baking sheet.

Heat pan and cook ground beef with garlic powder. Cook for 5 minutes.

While removing, season with salt and pepper.

In a bowl, mix all the sauce ingredients. Mix well until combined.

Spread nachos chips over the baking sheet. Top layer with ground beef and sauce.

Bake for 10 minutes.

Garnish with sesame seeds.

Mac nachos is ready.

Grilled Nachos

Grilled nachos is finger-licking good and perfect for summer cookouts. This recipe is tasty, cheesy and loaded with great toppings like black beans, cheese, tomatoes, onions, and sour cream.

Serving Size: 2

Cooking Time: 15 Minutes

Ingredients:

- 1/2 bag nachos chips
- 15 oz black beans, drained
- 2 tomatoes, chopped
- 4 oz jack cheese, shredded
- 3 green onions, chopped
- 1/4 cup sour cream
- Cooking oil, for spray

Instructions:

Heat grill on low heat.

Tear 18-inch long foil pieces and put them on the work surface. Keep their ends together.

Spray cooking oil over the foil.

Place nachos chips on the one side of a foil. Sprinkle, beans and tomatoes.

Sprinkle cheese at the end. Fold the foil twice to seal and put on the grill. Cook for 10 minutes.

Remove from grill. Open it and then sprinkle onions, and drizzle sour cream.

Grilled nachos is ready.

Apple Nachos

Apple nachos is sweet, tasty and chocolaty snack. It's loaded with apple slices, honey, chocolate sauce, peanut butter sauce, pumpkin seeds, coconut, and cinnamon.

Serving Size: 2-3

Cooking Time: 10minutes

Ingredients:

- ½ bag tortilla chips
- 2 apples, cut into thin slices
- 5 tbsp chocolate chips, divided
- 1 tbsp honey
- 1 tsp oil
- ¼ cup peanut butter
- 2 tbsp coconut, shredded
- 1 ½ tbsp pumpkin seeds
- ½ tsp cinnamon

Instructions:

Arrange nachos in the spiral pattern. Put apple slices on it.

In a bowl, add chocolate chips and oil and mix well. Put the bowl in the microwave for 15 seconds to melt. Keep it aside.

Microwave peanut butter for 15 seconds.

Drizzle chocolate sauce and peanut butter on the apple slices. Drizzle honey as well.

Garnish with coconut and pumpkin seeds.

Sprinkle cinnamon powder.

Apple nachos is ready.

Chipotle Nachos

Chipotle nachos is loaded with spicy and delicious sauce over nachos and black beans, onion, cherry tomatoes, pineapple salsa, and cilantro. It's a refreshing recipe with tangy, sweet, and spicy combination to fall in love with.

Serving Size: 4-6

Cooking Time: 20 Minutes

Ingredients:

- 1 bag nachos chips
- 2 cups chipotle sauce
- ½ cup cherry tomatoes, diced
- ⅓ cup black beans, cooked
- ½ cup pineapple salsa
- ¼ cup red onion, chopped
- ¼ cup cilantro, chopped

Instructions:

Spread nachos chips on the serving plate. Drizzle chipotle sauce over it. Put pineapple salsa over it. Put red onion, black beans, cherry tomatoes and cilantro.

Chipotle nachos is ready.

Keto Nachos

Keto nachos is the perfect snack pleasure for you. It's tasty, delicious and loaded with pork rinds and avocado slices. Garnished with sour cream, tomatoes, and green onions, this one is sure to add to your snack diet menu.

Serving Size: 2-4

Cooking Time: 45 minutes

Ingredients:

- 2 avocados, ripped
- 1/2 bag pork rinds
- 3 tsp cumin
- 1/2 tsp cayenne pepper
- 1 tsp garlic powder
- 1/2 tsp onion powder
- 1 tsp chili powder
- 1/2 cup Mexican blend cheeses, shredded
- 1/4 can diced tomatoes with green chilies
- 2 tbsp sour cream
- 1 jalapeño, sliced
- 1 green onion, chopped

Instructions:

In the food processor bowl, grind pork rinds and make crumb.

Put avocado slices on the parchment paper. Season with half of the seasonings like cumin, garlic powder, chili powder and cayenne pepper.

Season pork rind with half of the seasoning same as avocado slices.

Bake avocado slices and pork rinds in oven at 400°F for 20 minutes.

Once remove from oven, serve on the platter. Garnish with cheese, green chilies, green onion, and tomatoes.

Return to oven again and bake for 3 minutes.

Top with sour cream at the end.

Keto nachos is ready.

Steak Nachos

Steak nachos is an ultimate indulgence sprinkled with cheese, steak, veggies, and fresh cilantro. This epic nachos dish is a perfect weeknight dinner appetizer.

Serving Size: 8-10

Cooking Time: 35 minutes

Ingredients:

- 40 nachos chips
- 8 oz Mexican cheese blend, shredded
- 1 tbsp vegetable oil
- Salt & pepper, to taste
- 1/2 cup black beans, drained
- 1 lb. steak
- 1/2 cup sweet corn
- 1/3 cup red onion, diced
- 1 jalapeno, sliced
- 1 avocado, sliced
- 1 tomato, diced

For the cream

- 1/3 cup greek yogurt
- 1/2 cup cilantro
- 1/2 tsp cumin powder
- 1/2 tsp garlic powder
- 1 lemon, juiced

Instructions:

Preheat oven to 450°F.

In the food processor bowl, add all the cream ingredients and process until smooth paste.

Season steak with salt and pepper. Heat oil in the pan. Add steak and cook 5 minutes each side.

Remove from pan once cooked. Line baking sheet with foil paper. Grease with oil.

Spread nachos chips over it.

Top with Mexican cheese blend, black beans, red onion, and steak.

Bake in oven for 15 minutes.

Remove from oven. Garnish with jalapeno, tomatoes, and avocado and drizzle fresh cilantro.

Steak nachos is ready.

Veggie Nachos

Veggie nachos is loaded with amazing crunchy veggies, cheese, and extremely delicious avocado dip. It's a lovely nachos recipe with black beans, feta cheese, and some healthy vegetables. Serve with avocado dip and any kind of salsa to enjoy the awesome taste.

Serving Size: 6

Cooking Time: 25 minutes

Ingredients:

- 8 oz nachos chips
- 15 oz beans, cooked
- 4 oz cheddar cheese, shredded
- 4 oz Jack cheese, shredded
- 1 red bell pepper, chopped
- ⅓ cup feta cheese, crumbled
- Pickled jalapeños
- ⅓ cup green onions, chopped
- 2 radishes, chopped
- 2 tbsp cilantro, chopped

Instructions:

Preheat oven to 400°F. Line a parchment paper on the baking tray.

Spread nachos chips over it. Keep it aside.

Spread cooked beans, bell peppers, feta cheese, pickled jalapenos, and Monterrey jack cheese over nachos.

Bake for 10 minutes.

Once nachos are ready, top with radishes, cilantro and green onions.

Veggie nachos is ready.

Greek Chicken Nachos

Greek chicken nachos is a tasty snack recipe with chicken, pita bread and served with hummus. You can top nachos with many veggies like tomatoes, beetroots, onion, bell peppers, roasted chickpeas, and feta cheese.

Serving Size: 4

Cooking Time: 30 minutes

Ingredients:

- 1/2 lb. chicken ground chicken
- 1 tbsp olive oil
- Salt and pepper, to taste
- 1 package pita bread
- Hummus, as needed

Instructions:

Season chicken pieces with oil, salt and pepper. Coat well.

Add chicken to the pan and cook on medium heat. Cook for 5 minutes.

Remove chicken pieces from the pan.

Toast pita bread and slice it.

Layer nachos chips over pita bread slices on the serving platter.

Serve with hummus.

Greek chicken nachos is ready.

Chicken Bell Pepper Nachos

This recipe is a colorful dish with crunchy and juicy bell peppers topped on nachos with seasoned chicken breast, black beans, cheese, sour cream, jalapeno pepper, and cilantro. It's a complete snack dish to enjoy with your friends at home parties.

Serving Size: 1

Cooking Time: 5 minutes

Ingredients:

- 2 tbsp jalapeño pepper, chopped
- 8 oz chicken breast, boneless
- 1/4 cup Mexican-blend cheese, shredded
- 1/4 tsp garlic powder
- Salt and pepper, to taste
- 12 bell peppers, cut into strips
- 1/4 cup black beans, drained
- 1/3 cup salsa
- 1/4 tsp onion powder
- 1/4 cup sour cream
- 1 tbsp cilantro, chopped

Instructions:

Preheat oven to 375°F.

Line a baking sheet with foil paper.

Place chicken on the baking sheet and drizzle oil and season with salt and pepper. Toss well.

Seal the edges of foil around chicken.

Bake for 20 minutes.

Remove baking sheet from oven. Put bell peppers, around. Bake for 5 minutes more.

Transfer the cooked chicken in the bowl.

Shred with the use of fork.

Top with beans and cheese. Bake for another 3 minutes until cheese melts.

Garnish with sour cream, jalapeño pepper, and fresh cilantro.

Chicken bell peppers nachos is ready.

Irish Nachos

This recipe is a snackable dish made with interesting ingredients. It has potatoes, bacon, along with sour cream, cheese, veggies and nachos. This one will surely make you fall for it as it has salty, zesty, and delicious taste.

Serving Size: 4

Cooking Time: 55 minutes

Ingredients:

- 5 potatoes, sliced
- 1 package nachos chips
- 2 tbsp olive oil
- Salt and pepper, to taste
- 1 cup cheddar cheese, shredded
- 4 bacon strips
- 1 cup green onions, chopped
- 1 small cup sour cream
- 1 tomato, chopped
- 1 jalapeno, chopped

Instructions:

Soak potato slices in water for 10 minutes.

Preheat oven to 450°F.

Dry potato slices on the paper.

Transfer to the bowl. Season with salt, pepper.

Spread potato slices on the baking sheet. Bake for 20 minutes.

Cook bacon strips in the pan until becomes crunchy for 5-6 minutes.

Arrange potato slices in the skillet. Top with nachos, cheese, bacon, sour cream, tomatoes, and jalapeno.

Irish nachos is ready.

Beef Nachos

Beef nachos is filled with ground beef, tortilla chips, black olives, cheese, beans, tomatoes, and cilantro. It's a refreshing, unique and perfect baked perfection dish to enjoy. Top with sour cream and other likely topping ingredients.

Serving Size: 6

Cooking Time: 30 minutes

Ingredients:

- 1 lb. ground beef
- 1 taco seasoning
- 15 oz beans
- ½ cup corn
- ½ cup olives, sliced
- 1 package nachos chips
- ½ cup black beans
- ½ cup salsa
- 1 cup cheddar cheese, shredded
- 1 cup jack cheese, shredded
- Jalapenos, for topping
- Sour cream, for drizzling
- Cilantro, chopped for topping

Instructions:

Preheat oven to 400°F.

Heat skillet on medium heat cook ground beef. Add taco seasoning to it and season well.

Add nachos chips to the baking sheet pan. Spread evenly.

Top with beef, corn, olives, black beans, salsa, cheese, and jalapenos.

Bake for 15 minutes.

Top with sour cream, and cilantro.

Beef nachos is ready.

Chile Chicken Nachos

Chile chicken nachos is an ideal recipe with amazing layers of chicken mixture, corn mixture, tortilla chips, and cheese. It's a spicy compilation of ingredients with amazing ingredients.

Serving Size: 10

Cooking Time: 35 minutes

Ingredients:

- 2 tbsp olive oil
- 2 garlic cloves, chopped
- 1 red onion, chopped & divided
- 1 tbsp tomato paste
- 1 chipotle chile, chopped
- 3 cups chicken stock
- 1 tsp ground cumin
- Salt, to taste
- 1 rotisserie chicken meat, shredded
- 10 oz bags corn, drained
- 1 chile, chopped
- 8oz Cotija cheese, grated and divided
- Cooking oil spray
- 8 oz bags tortilla chips, divided
- 2lb. sharp cheddar cheese, shredded, divided
- Radishes, sliced
- Cilantro leaves, chopped
- 1 cup sour cream

Instructions:

Heat oil in the pan. Cook garlic cloves and onions for 5-6 minutes.

Add in tomato paste and cook for 2 minutes. Then add chipotle chile, chicken stock, cumin powder, and salt. Bring to boil.

Cover and cook for 30 minutes.

Preheat oven to 350°F.

Transfer the mixture to the blender. Blend until smooth paste.

Return the mixture to the pan and add in shredded chicken. Simmer for some time and season with salt to taste.

Remove the pan from heat.

Combine corn, chile, ¾ cup cheese, and remaining onion in the bowl. Season with salt.

Grease baking sheet with cooking oil. Spread nachos chips evenly. Top with chicken mixture, corn mixture, and cheese.

Bake for 10 minutes.

Chile chicken nachos is ready.

BBQ Chicken Nachos

BBQ chicken nachos have smoky flavors with cheese. It's a wow moment for people eating this loaded nachos recipe with chicken, cheese and topped with cilantro and avocado slices. It's a 30-minute crowd-pleaser recipe.

Serving Size: 4

Cooking Time: 25 minutes

Ingredients:

- 2 cups chicken, shredded
- 3/4 cups barbecue sauce, for marination
- 18 oz bag nachos chips
- 3 cup cheddar cheese, shredded
- 1 cup Cotija cheese, crumbled
- 1 cup pickled jalapeños
- 1/2 red onion, sliced
- 1 avocado, sliced
- Cilantro, chopped for garnishing

Instructions:

Preheat oven to 400°F. Line a baking sheet with foil paper.

In a bowl, combine BBQ sauce with chicken and toss well.

Spread nachos chips on the baking sheet. Then top with marinated chicken, cheddar cheese, cotija cheese, pickled jalapenos, and onion.

Bake for 15 minutes.

Remove from oven. Sprinkle cilantro and top with avocado slices.

BBQ chicken nachos is ready.

Mexican Nachos

Mexican nachos is a creamy snack dish with fresh and tangy ingredients. It's loaded with corn mixed with mayonnaise, chili powder, cilantro and cheese sauce. It has a cheesy mild and comforting taste.

Serving Size: 8

Cooking Time: 35 minutes

Ingredients:

- 2 tbsp olive oil
- 3 cups corn, frozen
- 2 tbsp mayonnaise
- 14 oz nachos chips
- 3 cups jack cheese, grated
- 1 tbsp cornstarch
- 1/2 cup cream
- 1/2 cup milk
- 1 clove garlic, minced
- 1/4 cup Cotija cheese, crumbled
- 1/8 tsp chipotle chili powder
- 2 tbsp sour cream
- 1/2 lime, wedges
- 2 tbsp cilantro, chopped

Instructions:

Heat oil in the pan. Add corn and cook until slight brown.

Transfer corn to the bowl and combine with mayonnaise.

Keep it aside.

Preheat oven to 350°F.

Spread nachos chips on the baking sheet. Bake for 10 minutes.

Melt jack cheese on the double boiler to make cheese sauce.

Then add cornstarch, sour cream, milk and garlic. Mix well.

The sauce is ready.

Transfer nachos chips on the platter. Drizzle cheese sauce.

Top with corn, cotija cheese, and sprinkle chipotle powder.

Sprinkle cilantro.

Serve with lime wedges.

Mexican nachos is ready.

Tuna Nachos

Tuna nachos is a rich snack that feels like a plan to paradise. It's fully loaded with tuna, radishes, avocado, onion, sriracha mayonnaise topped on nachos chips.

Serving Size: 4

Cooking Time: 40 minutes

Ingredients:

- 1 lb. tuna, cut into pieces
- 1.5tbsp lime juice
- ½ cup red onion, chopped
- 1 tbsp soy sauce
- ¾ cup mayonnaise
- 2 tbsp Sriracha
- 12 oz nachos chips
- 4 radishes, sliced
- 1 avocado, sliced
- 1 jalapeño, sliced
- ½ cup cilantro, chopped
- 1 lime, wedges

Instructions:

In the bowl, mix tuna, onion, lime juice, and soy sauce. Combine well. Keep it aside.

In another bowl, combine mayonnaise with sriracha.

Spread nachos chips on the platter. Spread tuna over it. Top with radishes, avocado, jalapeno, and cilantro. Then top with Sriracha mayonnaise over it.

Serve with lime wedges.

Tuna nachos is ready.

Fruit Nachos

Fruit nachos is an amazing reinvention to combine nachos and fruits on one platter. Replace the boring appetizers with these classic crispy chips, topped with tropical fruits and creamy coconut sauce.

Serving Size: 4

Cooking Time: 30 minutes

Ingredients:

- Cooking oil spray, for greasing
- 1 bag nachos chips
- ¼ cup sugar, divided
- ¼ tsp cinnamon
- ½ cup coconut milk
- Salt, to taste
- 1 tsp cornstarch
- 1 tbsp cold water
- 2 tsp lemon juice
- ½ cup pineapple, diced
- ½ cup mango, diced
- ½ cup strawberries, diced
- 1 kiwifruit, diced
- ¼ cup coconut flakes, toasted
- 2 tbsp mint leaves, sliced

Instructions:

Preheat oven to 400°F.

Coat baking sheet with cooking oil spray. Spread nachos chips on it.

In the bowl, mix sugar and cinnamon. Sprinkle the mixture over nachos chips.

Bake for 10 minutes.

In the saucepan, stir in coconut milk, half of the sugar, and salt. Mix well. Add cornstarch mixture to it and cook for a minute. Add in lemon juice and remove from pan.

In a large bowl, combine kiwi, strawberries, mango, pineapple and toss well.

Place nachos chips on the platter and top with fruit mixture.

Top with sauce, coconut flakes and mint leaves.

Fruit nachos is ready.

Bean Nachos

Enjoy this garlic and cumin bean mixture on the nachos chips. This whole recipe has a good amount of nutrition and tastes spicy and delicious. Perfect for an evening snack and best to serve your kids.

Serving Size: 6

Cooking Time: 25 Minutes

Ingredients:

- 12 -15 corn nachos
- Cooking oil, for greasing
- 1 tbsp canola oil
- 2 tsp cumin powder
- 1 tsp red chili powder
- 2 garlic cloves, minced
- 15 oz beans, undrained
- 1 cup white cheese, crumbled
- 1 cup salsa
- 1 cup avocado, diced
- 6 tbsp cilantro, chopped

Instructions:

Heat oil in the deep saucepan. Stir in cumin powder, red chili powder, and garlic and cook for 30-40 seconds.

Add beans to the saucepan and boil. Simmer for 10 minutes on low heat.

Then mash the beans. Spoon the bean mixture over nachos chips.

Top with cheese, salsa, and avocado. Sprinkle fresh cilantro on the top.

Bean nachos is ready.

Shrimp & Crabmeat Nachos

Shrimp & crabmeat nachos is a comforting and rich snack recipe with a lovely mixture of shrimp, crabmeat topped on tortilla chips. It tastes delicious and the melted cheese and pickled jalapeno taste greater.

Serving Size: 6-8

Cooking Time: 20 Minutes

Ingredients:

- 1 tsp olive oil
- 1 lb. shrimp, peeled
- 3 tsp cumin powder, toasted
- 1 tsp garlic, minced
- 1 lb. crabmeat
- ¾ cup sour cream
- 1 bunch green onions, sliced
- 9 oz nachos chips
- 3 cups jack cheese, grated
- ½ cup pickled jalapeño, sliced

Instructions:

Heat oil in the pan. Stir in shrimp, cumin powder and minced garlic. Cook for a minute.

In a bowl, mix cooked shrimp, crabmeat, sour cream, and green onions. Combine eveyrhting.

Spread nachos chips on baking sheet lined with foil paper. Put shrimp mixture evenly on chips.

Sprinkle jack cheese and put pickled jalapeno.

Broil for 5 minutes until cheese melts completely.

Shrimp nachos is ready.

Chicken Enchilada Nachos

Chicken enchilada nachos is tangy, tasty, and a game-changer. The enchilada sauce is the real essence of this dish mixed with chicken and herbs bring joy.

Serving Size: 4

Cooking Time: 40minutes

Ingredients:

For chicken and sauce

- 1 onion, cut into wedges
- 1 tbsp olive oil
- 10 oz enchilada sauce
- 1 cup tomatoes, crushed
- 15 oz black beans, drained
- 1 tsp oregano
- 1 chipotle chile, minced
- 1 tbsp brown sugar
- 2 cups chicken, shredded

For nachos

- 8 oz nachos chips
- 1.5 cups cheese, grated
- 2 cups lettuce, shredded
- ½ cup cilantro, chopped

Instructions:

Heat oil in the pan. Cook onion for 5 minutes.

Stir in enchilada sauce, tomatoes, beans, oregano, sugar and chipotle chile. Cook for 5 minutes on low heat. Add in chicken and cook for another 5 minutes. The chicken and sauce is ready.

Top nachos chips with chicken and sauce mixture, lettuce, cheese, and fresh cilantro.

Chicken enchilada nachos is ready.

Cowboy Nachos

Cowboy nachos is loaded with hot sauce, beef, beans, taco sauce and jack cheese. It's an all-time favorite and classic recipe serving savory appetizers. Enjoy this making at home and top with your favorite ingredients like guacamole, sour cream, jalapeno peppers.

Serving Size: 1

Cooking Time: 5 minutes

Ingredients:

- 16 oz beans, drained
- 2 tbsp hot sauce
- 1 tsp garlic, minced
- ½ tsp black pepper powder
- 3.5 cups beef brisket, shredded
- 1 tbsp canola oil
- ½ cup taco sauce
- 9 oz nachos chips
- 8 oz Jack cheese, shredded

Instructions:

Preheat oven to 450°F.

Heat oil in the saucepan. Add beans, garlic, black pepper powder, beef brisket to the pan. Cook for 7 minutes on medium heat.

Add in taco sauce and mix well. Cook for 2-3 minutes.

Spread nachos chips on the baking sheet. Put beef brisket mixture and cheese over it. Bake for 5 minutes.

Cowboy nachos is ready.

Chorizo Nachos

Chorizo nachos is a delicious pork topped on nachos with some adorning ingredients. It has amazing fresh flavors of avocado, cilantro, radishes and melted jack cheese creates a succulent appetizer.

Serving Size: 4

Cooking Time: 20 minutes

Ingredients:

- 1 ⅔ cups chorizo, cooked
- 1 cup beans, drained
- 8 corn nachos chips
- Cooking oil, for greasing
- 2 oz jack cheese, shredded
- 2 oz white cheese, crumbled
- ¼ cup green onions, chopped
- 1 cup tomato, chopped
- ¼ cup radishes, sliced
- ¼ cup cilantro, chopped
- 1 avocado, chopped
- 1 jalapeno pepper, sliced
- Salt, to taste

Instructions:

Preheat broiler.

In the saucepan, mix beans with chorizo and cook for 5-6 minutes.

Spread nachos chips in the baking sheet lined with foil paper and greased with oil.

Sprinkle onions, white cheese and jack cheese over chips. Broil for a minute until cheese melts completely.

Garnish with chorizo mixture, avocado, radishes, cilantro, jalapeno pepper, and salt to taste.

Chorizo nachos is ready.

Traditional Nachos

Want to go for something simple? This recipe brings you simple steps, home available ingredients and gets ready in just 20 minutes. It's a low-fat traditional nachos recipe with amazing taste buds.

Serving Size: 2

Cooking Time: 20 minutes

Ingredients:

- ½ cup chicken breast, shredded
- 1 oz nachos chip
- ¼ cup black beans
- 1 cup tomatoes and scallion, chopped
- 5 tbsp Mexican cheese blend, shredded

Instructions

Preheat oven to 400°F.

Arrange nachos chips on the baking sheet.

Top with chicken breast, black beans, tomatoes, scallions, and cheese blend.

Bake for 5 minutes.

Traditional nachos is ready.

Ravioli Nachos

Ravioli nachos is loaded with fried ravioli coated with breadcrumbs and egg mixture. These raviolis are topped on nachos chips and then topped with chicken, jack cheese, and other delicious toppings like guacamole, salsa, and cilantro tastes amazing.

Serving Size: 8

Cooking Time: 40 minutes

Ingredients:

- Cooking oil, for frying
- 2 eggs
- 1 tbsp Mexican hot sauce
- 1 tbsp water
- 1.5 cups breadcrumbs
- 40 cheese ravioli, frozen
- 1.5 cups grill chicken, diced
- 1.5 cups jack cheese, shredded
- ¼ cup sour cream
- 1 tbsp lemon juice
- 1 cup salsa
- ⅓ cup guacamole
- ⅓ cup cilantro leaves, chopped
- 3 tbsp black olives, sliced

Instructions:

Line baking sheet with foil paper.

Heat oil in the deep pot. Combine breadcrumbs, hot sauce, and water in the dish.

Mix ravioli with beat eggs mixture. And then coat in the breadcrumbs mixture.

Fry in the deep pot until golden brown for 3 minutes.

Preheat oven.

Transfer fried ravioli on the baking sheet. Top with chicken, and jack cheese. Broil for 2-3 minutes until cheese melts.

In a small bowl, combine sour cream and lemon juice. Top nachos with sour cream mixture, salsa, black olives, cilantro, and guacamole.

Ravioli nachos is ready.

Jackfruit Nachos

If you are in search of some amazing appetizers, then this jackfruit nachos will surely win your heart. This is a perfect recipe for game day and happy hour snacking with crunchy chips topped with jackfruit tossed in BBQ sauce, cheese, cilantro, jalapeno and sour cream.

Serving Size: 4

Cooking Time: 50 minutes

Ingredients:

- 20 oz jackfruit
- 1/2 onion, diced
- 1/2 cup BBQ sauce
- 8 oz nachos chips
- 2 cups cheddar cheese, shredded
- 1 tomato, sliced
- ½ red onion, diced
- 1 jalapeno, diced
- ¼ cup cilantro
- ¼ cup sour cream
- 1 lemon, wedges

Instructions:

Boil water in the big pot.

Add jackfruit to the pot. Boil for 30 minutes on medium to low heat. Once boiled, remove from pot. Shred with fork.

In a large bowl, add onion, jackfruit, and BBQ sauce. Toss well.

Preheat oven to 375°F.

Arrange nachos chips on the baking sheet. Top with jackfruit mixture and cheese. Bake for 5 minutes.

Top with jalapeno, red onion, sour cream, and cilantro. Serve with lemon wedges side.

Jackfruit nachos are ready.

Pie Crust Nachos

Pie crust nachos is crispy baked affair coated with sugar-cinnamon mixture and drizzle with chocolate syrup, colourful sprinkles and nuts. It's simple to make this recipe in less 30 minutes and kid's friendly.

Serving Size: 4-6

Cooking Time: 25 minutes

Ingredients:

- 9-inch pie crust, frozen
- 1/4 cup sugar
- 1 tsp cinnamon powder
- Chocolate syrup, for garnishing
- Sprinkles and nuts, for garnishing

Instructions:

Preheat oven to 350°F.

Line a baking sheet with parchment paper.

Slice pie crust into triangles shape like nachos.

Coat pie crust chips with sugar and cinnamon mixture.

Bake for 10 minutes until chips are crunchy.

Top with chocolate syrup, colorful sprinkles and nuts.

Pie crust nachos is ready.

Cajun Nachos

Cajun nachos is loaded with three-layer mixtures: Cajun black beans, Cajun sauce, and sausages. It's a heavy appetizer to enjoy along with your dinner with sweet, spicy and tangy affair. It's a wonderful dish with lots of ingredients poured on.

Serving Size: 6

Cooking Time: 35 minutes

Ingredients:

For black beans mixture

- ½ tbsp olive oil
- 15 oz black beans, rinsed
- 2 tbsp green onions, sliced
- ½ tsp hot sauce
- 1 tsp garlic, minced
- 1 tsp Cajun seasoning

For Cajun sauce

- ¾ cup sour cream
- 2 tbsp horseradish sauce
- 2 tsp tomato ketchup
- 1 tsp dill pickle juice
- ½ tsp paprika powder
- ¼ tsp cayenne pepper
- Salt and pepper, to taste

For nachos

- 16 oz sausage diced
- 1 cup jack cheese, shredded
- ½ cup cheddar cheese, shredded
- 8 cups nachos chips
- ¼ cup green onions, sliced
- ¼ cup jalapenos, sliced

- 1 tomato, diced

Instructions:

Heat oil in the pan. Add black beans, green onion, garlic, hot sauce and Cajun seasoning.

Sauté for 5 minutes.

Cajun black beans are ready.

In a mixing bowl, mix all the Cajun sauce ingredients. Cajun sauce is ready.

Preheat oven to 450°F.

Arrange nachos chips on the baking sheet.

Cook sausages in the pan for 10 minutes.

Top nachos with sausages, black beans, Cajun sauce, jack cheese, and cheddar cheese.

Bake for 5 minutes.

Cajun nachos is ready.

Fajita Nachos

Fajita nachos is simple and easy to make appetizer. The nachos chips are loaded with marinated steak, grilled veggies, salsa and sour cream. It's ready in less than 20 minutes and a tasty recipe.

Serving Size: 2-4

Cooking Time: 20 minutes

Ingredients:

- 1 lb. steak
- ¼ tsp cumin powder
- ¼ tsp cayenne
- 1 lemon, juiced
- 1.5 tbsp olive oil
- 4 oz peppers, cut into pieces
- 1 onion, diced
- 14 oz nachos chips
- ½ cup sour cream
- ½ cup salsa

Instructions:

Marinate steak with cumin powder, cayenne, and lemon juice, and olive oil.

Heat the grill pan and grill steak with peppers, and onions.

Spread nachos chips on the serving platter. Top with steak and grilled vegetables, salsa and sour cream.

Fajita nachos is ready.

Zucchini Nachos

Zucchini nachos is a healthier and light alternative to traditional nachos recipes. It has zucchini slices seasoned with spices, topped with nachos crisps, sour cream, chicken, and cheese.

Serving Size: 6

Cooking Time: 1 hour30 minutes

Ingredients:

- 2 zucchini, slices
- 1 pack nachos chips
- ½ tsp salt
- 1 tbsp olive oil
- ½ onion, chopped
- 1 lb. ground chicken
- 1 tsp chili powder
- ½ tsp paprika powder
- ½ tsp cumin powder
- ½ tsp garlic powder
- ½ tsp salt
- ¼ tsp dried oregano
- ¼ tsp black pepper powder
- 2 cups cheddar cheese, shredded
- ½ cup sour cream
- 3 green onions, chopped

Instructions:

Season zucchini with salt in a bowl.

Preheat oven to 400°F. Line baking sheet with butter paper.

Heat oil in the pan. Sauté onion for 5 minutes. Then add chicken and cook for another 5 minutes.

Add paprika powder, cumin powder, garlic powder, oregano, chili powder, salt and pepper. Mix well.

Arrange zucchini slices on the baking sheet. Bake for 5 minutes.

Serve zucchini slices on the platter. Top with cheese, and bake for another 2 minutes until cheese melts.

Serve nachos chips, sour cream, jalapeno, and green onions on the top.

Zucchini nachos is ready.

Pumpkin Nachos

Pumpkin nachos is healthier and loaded with seasoned pumpkins, black beans, cheese, and salsa on the tortilla chips. It's a simple-to-make recipe with a mild taste of pumpkin.

Serving Size: 12

Cooking Time: 45minutes

Ingredients:

- 4 cups pumpkin, cubed
- 2 tbsp olive oil
- Salt & pepper, to taste
- 13 oz nachos chips
- 15 oz black beans, rinsed
- 16 oz salsa
- 3 cups Mexican cheese blend, shredded

Instructions:

Preheat oven to 400°F.

Spread pumpkin in the baking pan. Drizzle oil and season with salt and pepper. Combine well. Roast for 30 minutes.

Arrange nachos chips. Top with pumpkin, salsa, black beans, and cheese. Bake for 5 minutes until cheese is melted.

Pumpkin nachos is ready.

Conclusion

If you have stale chips in your kitchen, we have found great ways to help you make something special. Get this 30 loaded cheesy nachos recipes cookbook that will help you make delicious recipes.

You can pick up a bag of tortillas and turn it into a rocking recipe with some sizzling ingredients like brisket, bacon steak, pork, and shredded chicken. This cookbook suggests a great bunch of appetizers, party snacks, and breakfast nachos as well.

Toppings ranging from vegetables, fruits, meat, nachos can be a simple yet appetizing recipe to throw all ingredients on the top of nachos.

Learn making these homemade nachos recipes from your kitchen!

Biography

"Cooking is a chore unless you love the process", which is the motto of Tyler Sweet, an extremely talented chef who has made her name in the catering industry with the help of her deep understanding of a variety of ingredients and human taste buds. She had always loved whipping up new recipes as a pass time activity but her career began when she got her first job at a local restaurant and realized that she would not mind doing it forever.

Tyler's hobby blossomed into a passion that drove her up the ladder so quickly that by the end of the year, she was already a sous chef and a rising talent. An impeccable eye for unique mixtures and a willingness to learn new dishes, she has since then worked for over 10 five-star restaurants in the tri-state. Presently, Sweet owns a thriving online cooking class where she has found a great, interactive avenue to teach on her most favorite subject, food.

Author's Note

I really appreciate you taking the time to not just download but also read my book, you don't know but that is the highest compliment you can ever give me. And it may seem greedy but I just have one more favor to ask of you, I need your feedback. Do you have any comments, suggestions, or complaints? Or you have an idea for my next book? Please reach out to me if you like, I'm always available for my loyal readers.

Thank you.

Tyler Sweet

Printed in Great Britain
by Amazon